Get set... GO!

Smell and Taste!

Ruth Thomson

Photographs by Peter Millard

Contents

Watts Books

London • New York • Sydney

What is smell?

Sniff some flowers.
Sniff deeply, using both nostrils.
As you sniff, you breathe in air.
The air contains minute particles
of the flower.

The particles hit hairy smell cells
that line the top of your nostrils.
You have about ten million smell cells.

The cells send signals to the brain.
The brain works out
that the smell is a flowery one.

Your sense of smell helps you enjoy
the taste of food and other things around you.
It can also warn you of bad food,
smoke or poisonous fumes.

Describing smells

Get ready

- ✔ Minty sweet
- ✔ Curry powder
- ✔ Shoe polish
- ✔ Aftershave
- ✔ Flowers
- ✔ Dirty sock
- ✔ Cheese
- ✔ Damp soil
- ✔ Vinegar

...Get set

Smell each thing in turn.

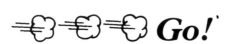 **Go!**

What happens if you sniff deeply?
What happens if you wrinkle up your nose?
Think of words to describe each smell.
Is it fragrant, sharp or musty?
Is it fresh, mouldy or flowery?

Smell in the dark

Get ready

✔ Coffee ✔ Chocolate ✔ Mint

✔ Onion (cut) ✔ Orange (cut) ✔ Soap

✔ Lemon (cut) ✔ Cheese ✔ Honey

...Get set

Ask a friend to shut his eyes.
Let him sniff one thing at a time.

⇶⇶⇶ *Go!*

Can he guess what the things are?
If he gets stuck, first give him a clue,
then let him look at the things.
Do hearing and seeing help
his sense of smell?

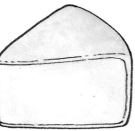

What a pong!

Get ready

✔Ground coffee   ✔Garlic (crushed)   ✔Perfume

...Get set

Press one nostril completely shut.
Sniff the coffee with your other nostril
for at least half a minute.

≈✿≈✿≈✿ Go!

Does the smell get stronger or weaker,
the longer you sniff?
Press the open nostril shut
and sniff with the other one.
How strong is the smell now?
Now smell the perfume or garlic.
How strong are their smells?

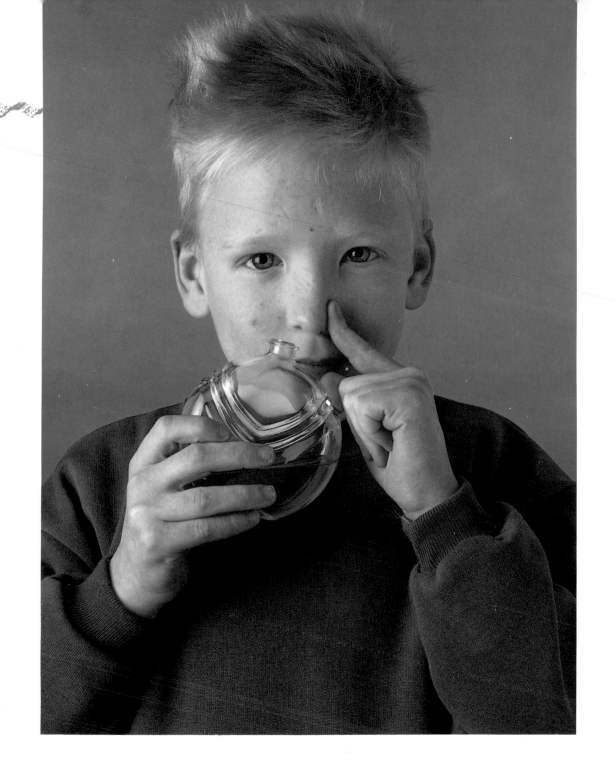

What is taste?

Look at your tongue in a mirror.
Can you feel and see bumps on it?
Lining those bumps are tiny taste buds.

Taste buds respond to whatever you eat.
They send signals to the brain.
The brain works out
what the tastes are.

There are four basic tastes –
sweet, sour, salt and bitter.
Taste buds on different parts
of your tongue respond
to each taste.

Your sense of taste protects you
from eating bad or harmful foods.
Their awful taste makes you spit them out.

A taste map

Get ready

- ✔ Paper
- ✔ Felt-tip pens
- ✔ Lemon juice
- ✔ Sugary water
- ✔ Salty water
- ✔ Black coffee
- ✔ Glass of cold water
- ✔ Cotton buds

...Get set

Dip a cotton bud in lemon juice.
Dab it on different parts of your tongue.
Do the same with the other tastes.
Sip water before you try a new taste.

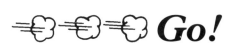 **Go!**

Where can you taste most of the tastes?
Where can you taste nothing?
Where can you taste bitter things best?
Draw a taste map of your tongue.

Bitter

Sour

Salty

Sweet

Tastes juicy

Get ready

✔ Plastic spoon ✔ Metal spoon ✔ Glass

✔ Sugar lump ✔ Apple ✔ Biscuit

...Get set

Lick the glass and the two spoons.
Now lick the sugar lump, the apple
and the biscuit.

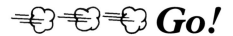 **Go!**

Which of them can you taste?

Things have to dissolve in the juices
in your mouth, known as saliva,
before you can taste them.
Glass, metal and plastic do not dissolve
in saliva, so they are tasteless.

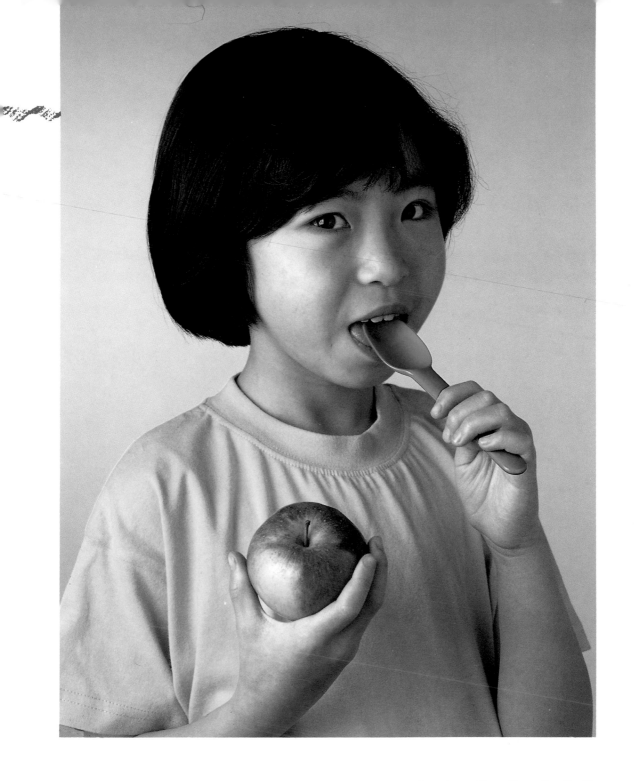

Warm and cold

Get ready

- ✔ 3 glasses
- ✔ Lemon
- ✔ Ice cubes
- ✔ Sugar
- ✔ Coffee
- ✔ Water
- ✔ Salt
- ✔ Teaspoon

...Get set

Mix two teaspoons of sugar with hot water.
Put some of the mixture into each glass.
Add cold water to one of the glasses.
Put ice cubes and cold water in another.
Add warm water to the third one.

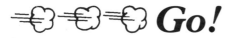 **Go!**

Sip each drink. Does heat affect its taste?
Make and taste similar salt, coffee and
lemon juice mixtures.
Are the results the same?

 # How does it taste?

Get ready

✔ Apple ✔ Onion ✔ Banana

✔ Parsnip ✔ Potato

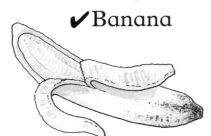

...Get set

Ask a grown-up to peel and cube the foods.
Shut your eyes and hold your nose.
Chew each food in turn.

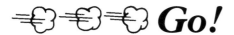 ### *Go!*

Can you tell which food is which?
Taste them again, with your nose unblocked.
What happens to their tastes now?
What happens if you smell the apple
as you eat the parsnip?

Aftertastes

Get ready

✔ Chocolate   ✔ Toothpaste   ✔ Glass of
✔ Glass of   ✔ Glass of   cold water
    salty water   orange juice

...Get set

Eat some chocolate, then sip salty water.
Taste some toothpaste.
then sip orange juice.

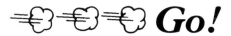 **Go!**

When you eat strongly-flavoured food,
what happens to the taste
of the next food or drink you take?
What happens if you take a sip
of plain water between each taste?

20

Tasting colours

Get ready

✔ Cold milk ✔ Food colourings ✔ Glasses

...Get set

Pour milk into several glasses.
Add drops of different food colouring.
Ask a friend to sip each drink.

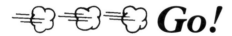 **Go!**

What flavour does she think
each glass of milk tastes of?
Which flavour does she like best and least?

Food colouring is actually tasteless.
What you think a drink tastes like
depends on its look as well as its smell.

22

Index

Words that appear in *italics* describe the ideas behind the activities.

aftertaste 20

banana 18
brain 2, 10
bitter tastes 10, 12, 16

chocolate 6, 20
coffee 6, 8, 12, 16
cotton buds 12

describing smells 4
dirty sock 4

flowers 2, 4
food colouring 22

garlic 8

lemon juice 12, 16

milk 22

nostrils 2, 8, 18

onion 6, 18
orange juice 20

perfume 8

saliva 14
sense of smell 2
sense of taste 10
smell cells 2

smelling –
  with eyes shut 6
  with one nostril 8
sour tastes 10, 12
sweet tastes 10, 12

taste buds 10
taste map 12
tongue 10, 12
toothpaste 20
tasting –
  cold drinks 16
  different colours 22
  warm drinks 16
  with nose blocked 18

Acknowledgments:
The author and publisher would like to thank the pupils of Kenmont Primary School, London, for their participation in the photographs of this book.
Photographic credits:
Chris Fairclough 3.

©1994 Watts Books

Watts Books
96 Leonard Street
London EC2A 4RH

Franklin Watts Australia
14 Mars Road
Lane Cove
NSW 2066

UK ISBN 0 7496 1674 1
10 9 8 7 6 5 4 3 2 1

Series Editor: Pippa Pollard
Editor: Annabel Martin
Design: Ruth Levy
Cover design: Nina Kingsbury
Artwork: Ruth Levy

A CIP catalogue record for this book is available from the British Library

Dewey Decimal Classification
612.8

Printed in Malaysia